THE TIMELESS ART

OF ALLOWING BOOKS TO THRIVE

Robert Bringhurst

in conversation with

Ulises Carrión

CODE(X)+1 MONOGRAPH
NUMBER 11

Copyright © 2015 by the Codex Foundation
ISBN: 978-0-9962184-1-2

Number 11 in the CODE(X)+1 monograph series published by:

THE CODEX FOUNDATION
2203 Fourth Street, Berkeley, California 94710
www.codexfoundation.org

Distributed to the trade by Oak Knoll Books
www.oakknoll.com

500 copies were printed by Peter Rutledge Koch
with the assistance of Jonathan Gerken and Dina Pollack.

PREFACE

Ulises Carrión was born in southern Veracruz on 29 January 1941. He studied literature and languages at the Universidad Autónoma de México, the Sorbonne, and the University of Leeds before settling in Amsterdam in the early 1970s. Early in his career, he wrote experimental poetry and short fiction. Later, he grew more and more preoccupied with radio, video, avant-garde film, an aleatory and collaborative amusement known as mail art, the organization of counter-cultural festivals, and with the making and exhibiting of mostly low-budget, self-published "artists' books." He died of AIDS in Amsterdam at the age of 48, on 6 October 1989.

In some circles at least, he is now remembered more for his writing about art than for any art he made. One example is the lively and aphoristic essay called "El arte nuevo de hacer libros" – The New Art of Making Books – written in Amsterdam in May 1974. The title recalls another equally stylish and irreverent dissertation: Lope de Vega's verse essay "El arte nuevo de hacer comedias en este tiempo," delivered as an address to a boisterous private salon that met in Madrid in the early 1600s. Lope included that essay in the 1609 edition of his poems, and students of Spanish literature have studied it ever since. The literary allusion is typical of Carrión; so is the fact that the allusion is wholly unpretentious and casual, not in any sense a ticket of admission.

Carrión's kind of art has not lacked for proponents and exponents in the academy or in the art world, but much that has been written along these lines is intellectually murky and burdened with pompous jargon. Carrión himself, by contrast, was plain-spoken and full of real ideas. My own predilections are different from his, and so we disagree on many fronts, yet he is lucid and articulate – and therefore someone I can talk to, dead or alive.

His essay first appeared in the February 1975 issue of the monthly magazine *Plural*, which was the literary supplement of the once-great Mexican daily *Excélsior*. (*Plural* was founded in 1971 by Octavio Paz. Carrión contributed to it frequently during the early 1970s, when *Excélsior* was owned by its own employees, edited by the legendary Julio Scherer, and widely known as "*Le Monde* de México." In 1976, when Scherer was forced out, the paper's stature started to sink, and many Mexican intellectuals and writers, including Carrión, vanished from its pages.) Newspapers are fugitive media, but papers as good as *Excélsior* once was are not so easily

3

forgotten. Carrión's essay was read and discussed with some excitement in Mexico and beyond. Photocopies were passed from hand to hand, and it was published before long in English, Polish, French, and German. Nearly all of these editions were produced out of pure, uncommercial enthusiasm by small presses or counter-cultural galleries. In 1977 the piece appeared in the anti-establishment San Francisco periodical *Art Contemporary*. In 1980 it was included in *Second Thoughts*, a brief collection of Carrión's writings in English translation, published by Void Distributors, a collective in Amsterdam. Forty years after its first publication, it is still reappearing, in anthologies, exhibition catalogues, and independent chapbook editions in multiple languages. It merits the attention. It merits an engaged response as well.

Carrión's side of the conversation is printed here in roman, mine in italic – and to those who have read him in English before, Carrión's voice should sound familiar. For the most part, the English translation is the one he made himself in Amsterdam in 1976. But that translation was, in spots, less idiomatic and clear than the Spanish original. This time around, the English matches the Spanish more closely.

— R. B.

WHAT IS A BOOK?

A book is a sequence of spaces.

> *The empty shell of a book is a sequence of spaces, but no one with a working mind and heart writes or reads an empty shell. What animates the book?*

Each of these spaces is perceived at a different moment – a book is also a sequence of moments.

> *Yes. And often the temporal energy in a book is greater than the spatial.*

A book is not a case of words, nor a bag of words, nor a bearer of words.

> *Nor just a string of spaces either.*

·

A writer, contrary to popular opinion, does not write books.

> *You are trying to steal the book from the writer.*

A writer writes texts.

> *I was wrong. You're trying to BUY the book from the writer – for 26 letters and a handful of typewriter keys.*

The fact that a text is contained in a book comes only from the dimensions of such a text; or, in the case of a series of short texts (poems, for instance), from their number.

> *To a writer, 'text' is a generally charmless and technical term. A text is sliced and deep-fried literature, like potato chips. What matters is that the book can be a home for the flesh and blood of ideas, stories, music, speaking voices. Those things are known by a familiar nickname: words.*

·

A literary (prose) text contained in a book ignores the fact that the book is an autonomous space-time sequence.

> *It may seem to ignore it. Actually, it revels in that fact and takes full advantage of it. A real work of literature gives that space-time sequence cause to sing. It even supplies the words for the song.*

A series of more or less short texts (poems by various authors) distributed through a book following any particular ordering reveals the sequential nature of the book.

> I agree that deer prints are interesting. But are they more interesting (or better to eat) than the deer?

It reveals it, perhaps uses it; but it does not incorporate it or assimilate it.

> Quite so. But people don't ordinarily incorporate or assimilate the house in which they live. Nor, we hope, does the house assimilate them. The basic function of a book is to house a work of literature: to give it protection and some elbow room.

·

Written language is a sequence of signs expanding within space, the reading of which occurs in time.

> Yes. But everything that matters about those sequences of signs occurs in the mind, which is not so easy to locate in space and time.

A book is a space-time sequence.

> Yes. But the intelligence, where books and readers interact, is something more.

·

Books existed originally as containers of literary texts.

> Evidently there were account books long before there were literary books, and scribes were keeping inventories long before there was anyone writing down literature. But let's not quibble. What makes books important is their content; and what makes books amazing is their ability to carry sculpted voices – works of literature – great distances through space and time. So I applaud your statement in principle, though as history it is faulty.

But books, seen as autonomous realities, can contain any (written) language, not only literary language, or even any other system of signs.

> Sure. They can contain financial statements, lists of names and telephone numbers, records of baptisms and burials, stamp collections, house plans, the scores of string quartets or sonatas, magnificent photographs, patterns for making kimonos or neckties....

·

Among languages, literary language (prose and poetry) is not the best
fitted to the nature of books.

> *Literature was oral before it was written, so literary language is older – many times
> older – than physical books. But it adapted readily to books. Books have adapted to it
> too. They seem to me to fit together remarkably well. Why do you think otherwise?*

·

A book may be the accidental container of a text, the structure of which is
irrelevant to the book: these are the books of bookshops and libraries.

> *And tables can be the accidental bearers of dishes and glasses, bread and wine, or of
> notebooks and love letters, musical scores, vases of flowers. And chairs the accidental
> bearers of humans who are eating, talking, thinking, dreaming. Are you going to
> tell me that you've discovered the inner truth of tables and chairs, which we've been
> wasting or misusing all these years?*

A book can also exist as an autonomous and self-sufficient form, including
perhaps a text that emphasizes that form, a text that is an organic part of
that form: here begins the new art of making books.

> *Fine! But this new art is as old as Lascaux. We've had some time to see what it can do.
> Do you still really think that a story or poem can grow out of a book as fruitfully as a
> book can grow around a poem?*

·

In the old art the writer believes himself not to be responsible for the real
book. He writes the text. The rest is done by the servants, the artisans, the
workers, the others.

> *In the really old art, the oral poet was wholly responsible for the book. The mythteller
> made it – out of a mouthful of air, as a later poet said. After humans learned to write,
> scribes could transcribe what the mythtellers said. Then some of them learned to tell
> stories and sing with their pens. They turned into writers. Later still, yes, there were
> typographers, printers, binders. Artisans and craftsmen, not servants. And in that
> elaboration, the book thrived! But yes, mass-production has also cheapened it.*

In the new art writing a text is only the first link in the chain going from
the writer to the reader. In the new art the writer assumes responsibility
for the whole process.

Splendid — so long as the writer is willing and able to learn the crafts involved. Some have. In the old days, many writers were fine calligraphers. More recently, some have also learned typography, printing, and binding. But why are you opposed to specialization? Why shouldn't writers write, and engravers engrave, typographers do typography, printers print, and binders bind? What's wrong with having many connected arts instead of one? Does a pianist have to make her own piano?

•

In the old art the writer writes texts.

That's like saying musicians play notes. Not many musicians see it that way. Writers write what they can — poems, plays, stories, essays, letters — because writers have something to say, not in order to fill up the page.

In the new art the writer makes books.

What musicians actually do — and have always done — is make music. What writers do — and will keep on doing — is to make literature. If the writer makes literature on a large enough scale, then the writer makes books, just as a composer makes a concerto.

•

To make a book is to actualize its ideal space-time sequence by means of the creation of a parallel sequence of signs, be it verbal or other.

It sounds as if, for you, the book is bound before it is written. As if the pages come first, and the words, if there are any words, are called out of the air by the physical book. Why do you make the man-made object king?

PROSE AND POETRY

In an old book all the pages are the same.

Look more closely. Listen to what the words and pages say.

When writing the text, the writer followed only the sequential laws of language, which are not the sequential laws of books.

Are the laws of books deeper or better or more important than other laws — the inner principles of thinking and dreaming, for instance, or the laws (if you like to call them that) of syntax, harmony and counterpoint?

Words might be different on every page; but every page is, as such, identical with the preceding ones and with those that follow.

> *Like footprints. Like sunsets. Like mouthfuls of air. If you think that every time the sun goes down behind the mountain, or your foot comes down on the ground, or your pencil comes down on the page, it is senseless repetition, then I say you have somehow momentarily forgotten what it is to be alive.*

In the new art every page is different; every page is an individualized element of a structure (the book), in which it has a particular function to fulfill.

> *I can see the attraction, like sparkling lights. But what does this new art offer to people with longer memories and attention spans?*

•

In spoken and written language pronouns substitute for nouns, in order to avoid tiresome, superfluous repetitions.

> *Useful things, pronouns. Most human languages have them. In some literary traditions they're used very sparingly, in others profusely.*

In the book, composed of various elements, of signs, such as language, what is it that plays the role of pronouns, in order to avoid tiresome, superfluous repetitions?

> *Skillful repetition isn't superfluous or tiresome. In the fine old art of oral literature, just as in music, certain kinds of repetition are highly prized. But it has to be intelligent and organic, not mechanical, repetition.*

This is a problem for the new art; the old does not even suspect its existence.

> *I wonder if the old art is as brainless, or the new art as sagacious, as you say.*

•

A book of 500 pages, or of 100 pages, or even of 25, in which all the pages are similar, is a boring book considered as a book, no matter how thrilling the content of the words of the text printed on the pages might be.

> *No more boring than a vineyard or an orchard or a cornfield. The only books that are genuinely boring are those that are boring to read.*

A novel, by a writer of genius or by a third-rate author, is a book where nothing happens.

> *Very little needs to happen in the book. The idea is to make things happen in the mind – and maybe then in life as well.*
>
> •

There are still, and always will be, people who like reading novels. There will also always be people who like playing chess, gossiping, dancing the mambo, or eating strawberries with cream.

•

In comparison with novels, where nothing happens, in poetry books something happens sometimes, although very little.

> *Visually, nothing much happens in the script of King Lear, but if you put the script to use, things will happen on the stage. And if you watch the play – or if you merely read the book! – things will happen in your mind.*
>
> •

A novel with no capital letters, or set in different fonts, or with chemical formulae interspersed here and there, etc., is still a novel, that is to say, a boring book pretending not to be such.

> *A great novel can be as smooth as the surface of a great river. Underneath that surface, lots of water or emotion can be moving. Lots of ideas too, or lots of fish.*
>
> •

A book of poems contains as many, or more, words than a novel, but fundamentally it uses the real, physical space in which these words appear, in a way that is more intentional, plainer, and more profound.

> *Ulises, are you reading, or just looking?*

This is so because in order to transcribe poetic language onto paper it is necessary to translate typographically the conventions proper to poetic language.

> *Poetry can be transcribed as simply as prose. But many poets since Mallarmé have tried to map both speech and thought in the typographic silence of the page. Is that the*

source of the problem? Is it actually the poets who have led you and others to think of the book in such fervently materialistic terms?

•

The transcription of prose needs few things: punctuation, capitals, various margins, etc.

What it really needs is an ear. Good prose is as oral as good poetry.

All these conventions are original and extremely beautiful discoveries, but we don't notice them any more because we use them daily.

Quite true. Yet there are also those who notice them more and more – and for exactly the same reason: because they use them daily.

Transcription of poetry, a more elaborate language, uses less common signs. The mere need to create the signs fitting the transcription of poetic language, calls our attention to this very simple fact: to write a poem on paper is a different action from writing it in the mind.

I think most poetry is written with the voice, which is a link between the body and the mind. And sometimes, then, it is transcribed onto paper.

•

Poems are songs, the poets repeat. But they don't sing them. They write them.

All too true.

Poetry is to be said aloud, they repeat. But they don't say it aloud. They publish it.

Indeed, too many do.

The fact is that poetry, as it occurs normally, is written and printed, not sung or spoken, poetry. And with this, poetry has lost nothing.

Nothing but its sense of itself. Nothing but its purchase on the world. Nothing but its voice.

On the contrary, poetry has gained something: a spatial reality that the so loudly lamented sung and spoken poetries lacked.

What is it about space that makes you trust it more than time?

SPACE

For years, many years, poets have intensively and efficiently exploited the spatial possibilities of poetry.

> *They've worked to develop a spatial notation. So have musicians. But the space in which music and poetry actually happen is not the space of the page. The space in which they actually unfold is mental and auditory space, the space of time.*

But only the so-called concrete or, later, visual poetry, has openly declared this.

> *Is there such a thing as concrete poetry, or is it really a sportive form of graphic design?*

> •

Verses ending halfway on the page, verses having a wider or narrower margin, verses being separated from the following one by a bigger or smaller space – all this is exploitation of space.

> *Yes – in the interest of making a map of prosodic time. Noetic and visceral time.*

> •

This is not to say that a text is poetry because it uses space in this or that way, but that using space is a characteristic of written poetry.

> *Using space in this way is characteristic of* SOME *poetry – or some transcriptions of poetry, yes. But the interrelations of poetry and time are deeper and wider.*

> •

Space is the music of the unsung poetry.

> *Verbal music, like instrumental music, can be represented, imperfectly, in space, but time is where it happens. Spatial music is something else – architecture, we usually call it. But not even architecture can flourish without time.*

> •

The introduction of space into poetry (or rather of poetry into space) is an enormous event of literally incalculable consequences.

> *Maybe so. But Homer, Sophocles, Dante, Shakespeare, Goethe, Yeats, Rilke, García Lorca, and Neruda, whose art is vocal rather than spatial, are just as good as they ever were.*

One of these consequences is concrete and/or visual poetry. Its birth is not an extraneous event in the history of literature, but the natural, unavoidable development of the spatial reality gained by language since the moment writing was invented.

> *These are extravagant claims.*

•

The poetry of the old art does use space, albeit bashfully.

> *All thinking occupies space – at least a little space – but mostly it occupies time.*

This poetry establishes an intersubjective communication.

> *Things have always been able to talk to each other in literature. That is one of the things mythologies are for: giving images, ideas, voices, and other things room to make themselves heard.*

Intersubjective communication occurs in an abstract, ideal, impalpable space.

> *It occurs wherever we don't prevent it from doing so – wherever we don't wall reality off from itself.*

•

In the new art (of which concrete poetry is only an example) communication is still intersubjective, but it occurs in a concrete, real, physical space: the page.

•

A book is a volume in space.

> *Open the door of the book and you'll find that, if it has content, it occupies far less space than time. Minimal space, in fact, and maximal time.*

It is the true ground of the communication that takes place through words – its here and now.

> *Has speech disappeared? Has writing made talk obsolete?*

Concrete poetry represents an alternative to poetry.

> *Letters of the world, unite! Throw off the hegemony of words, sentences, paragraphs, songs, stories, voices!*

Books, regarded as autonomous space-time sequences, offer an alternative to all existing literary genres.

> *I accept that architecture is an art. But a house, no matter how fond of it you may be, is not an alternative or successor to the life of its inhabitants. Books are houses for works of literature, and houses for ideas, not replacements for them.*

•

Space exists outside subjectivity.

> *Everything that exists does so outside subjectivity.*

If two subjects communicate in the space, then space is an element of this communication. Space modifies this communication. Space imposes its own laws on this communication.

> *Yes.*

Printed words are imprisoned in the matter of the book.

> *Every reader who knows the language of that book can set them free. And still they remain there, like the magic food that is eaten yet not consumed.*

•

What is more meaningful: the book or the text it contains?
What was first: the chicken or the egg?

> *Long before there was the chicken or the egg there was life, which both chicken and egg embody. Long before there were physical books or written texts there was literature.*

•

The old art assumes that printed words are situated in an ideal space.

> *A pleasant and hopeful assumption — like the hope that a storyteller's language will be understood, and that she will be free to tell her story without being shot, shouted down, or clonked on the head.*

The new art knows that books exist as objects in an exterior reality, subject to concrete conditions of perception, existence, exchange, consumption, use, etc.

> *I think the old-time writers knew this too.*

•

The objective manifestation of language can be experienced in an isolated moment and space – the page; or in a sequence of spaces and moments – the 'book.'

> *I know that Amsterdam is full of newspaper vendors and bookshops – but it is also full of cafés and conversations. I don't mean to pry, but were you lonely when you wrote this? It's as if you'd lost faith in all forms of language other than writing.*

•

There is not and will not be new literature any more.

> *Have there not been any new poems, novels, or essays these past forty years? So far, the future has not been so bleak as you say.*

There will be, perhaps, new ways to communicate that will include language or will use language as a basis.

> *Indeed, a quarter century after your death, what you say has come to pass. But the old methods – talking and writing – are still going strong. Indeed, the new ways draw their strength from the old. Only their weaknesses are new.*

As a medium of communication, literature will always be old literature.

> *Real literature aspires to be timeless: neither old nor new. But it keeps being born.*

LANGUAGE

Language transmits ideas, i.e., mental images.

> *Yes – and a good deal more besides.*

The starting point of the transmission of mental images is always an intention: we speak to transmit a particular image.

> *We have in English a proverb: How do I know what I think till I see what I say? One can begin with the intention not of transmitting a certain image but of looking at things and asking what they mean.*

Everyday language and the old art language have this in common: both are intentional, both want to transmit certain mental images.

> *Only that?*

•

In the old art the meanings of the words are the bearers of the author's intentions.

> *This seems to me a poor description of what happens in Shakespeare's sonnets or in Moby-Dick. It's poorer still as a description of Finnegans Wake.*

As the ultimate meaning of words is indefinable, so the author's intention is unfathomable.

> *Suppose the author's intention is to see what he can learn, to clarify his vision and his language by testing each against the other, and both against reality?*

•

Every intention presupposes a purpose, a utility.

> *Prof. Kant had something to say on that subject. Purposeless purpose, or something to that effect. Intention with no particular intent. Some people have suggested that this is the essence of life as well as art.*

Everyday language is intentional, that is, utilitarian; its function is to transmit ideas and feelings, to explain, to declare, to convince, to invoke, to accuse, etc.

> *Often its function is just to sing, or to honor, or to praise. To celebrate the fact that there is someone rather than no one, something rather than nothing.*

Old art's language is intentional as well, i.e., utilitarian. Both languages differ from one another only in their form.

> *Hereabouts, we say that a lot depends on a red wheelbarrow glazed with rain and a few white chickens. No one has to intend this; it happens.*

•

New art's language is radically different from daily language. It neglects intentions and utility, and it returns to itself, it investigates itself, looking for forms, for series of forms that give birth to, couple with, unfold into, space-time sequences.

Do you then, in the new art, test language against itself and nothing more?

•

The words in a new book are not the bearers of a message, nor the mouthpieces of the soul, nor the currency of communication.

You're describing the difference between literature and non-literature, not between old literature and new.

Hamlet, an avid reader of books, had them pegged already: words, words, words.

•

The words of the new book are there not to transmit certain mental images with a certain intention.

Fine. But if what they do transmit is the artist's ceaseless consciousness of her own activity, or consciousness of her consciousness, what have we gained?

They are there to form, together with other signs, a space-time sequence that we identify with the name 'book.'

Words, letters, and numbers all exist for the sake of the physical book?

•

The words in a new book might be the author's own words or someone else's words.

Words are not privately owned. Writing, like speaking, consists in arranging existing words in certain new sequences, with certain rhythms and intonations, just as playing the piano consists in touching existing keys.

A writer of the new art writes very little or does not write at all.

Will dancers also cease to dance and musicians to play?

•

The most beautiful and perfect book in the world is a book with only blank pages, in the same way that the most complete language is that which lies beyond all that the words of a man can say.

> *This is an excellent place to start, and an excellent place to finish. In between, though, we do a lot of reaching for the things we can't quite say. Some of the reaching is beautiful too.*

·

Every book of the new art is searching after that book of absolute whiteness, in the same way that every poem searches for silence.

> *If so, then the new art is exemplary.*

·

Intention is the mother of rhetoric.

> *Lucidity is the mother of clear speech, and intention can be quite lucid. I'd say the mother of a lot of rhetoric is ambition – especially an ambition to inflate the self. I'd also say the father of a lot of rhetoric is fear.*

·

Words cannot avoid meaning something, but they can be divested of intentionality.

> *Again, Prof. Kant has beat you to it. And Lǎo Zi as well.*

·

A non-intentional language is an abstract language: it doesn't refer to any concrete reality.

> *What do you have against reality?*

Paradox: in order to be able to manifest itself concretely, language must first become abstract.

·

Abstract language means that words are not bound to any particular intention; that the word 'rose' is neither the rose that I see nor the rose that a more or less fictional character claims to see.

This is one of the basic principles of literature, yes – and always has been.

In the abstract language of the new art the word 'rose' is the word 'rose.' It means all the roses and it means none of them.

And in the concrete language of the old art too – unless the writer or storyteller causes it to be otherwise and makes a quite specific rose appear.

•

How to succeed in making a rose that is not my rose, nor his rose, but everybody's rose, i.e., nobody's rose?

By saying what you mean and meaning what you say.

By placing it within a sequential structure (for example a book), so that it momentarily ceases being a rose and becomes essentially an element of the structure.

Ah. You expect the book to save you. What do you want it to save you FROM?

STRUCTURES

Every word exists as an element of a structure – a phrase, a novel, a telegram.

Every word employed in literature, yes. But don't words also exist as potentials, like keys on the piano and nails in the bag?

Or: every word is part of a text.

Every word is part of a text when it's part of a text. Every word is also part of the word hoard, independent of any text. But words by themselves don't amount to very much. By themselves, they don't constitute language.

•

Nobody and nothing exists in isolation: everything is an element of a structure.

Yes. But some structures are a lot more structural than others. The structure of a tree, for instance, or a forest, is deeper than the structure of a woodpile.

Every structure is in its turn an element of another structure.

> *A potent point. But again, there are nesting structures that will take your breath away and others that will not.*

Everything that exists is a structure.

•

To understand something is to understand the structure of which it is a part and/or the elements forming the structure that that something is.

> *That's part of understanding.*

A book consists of various elements, one of which might be a text.

> *Yes.*

A text that is part of a book isn't necessarily the most essential or important part of that book.

> *In a book of Ansel Adams's photographs, you can pretty much skip the words. It would be better, in a case like that, to say the photos ARE the text. And they are crucial to that book. A cheap, readable paperback edition of Moby-Dick or Neruda's Odas elementales is far more valuable than a luxurious edition of a pompous or trivial text. And a book with nothing on the pages is an empty shell. So it doesn't seem to me that the text is irrelevant to the book.*

•

A person may go to the bookshop to buy ten red books because this color harmonizes with the other colors in his sitting room, or for any other reason, thereby revealing the irrefutable fact that books have a color.

> *Yes, but you are not describing a reader. A reader would buy ten books worth reading, not ten red ones. Who are books for?*

•

In a book of the old art words transmit the author's intention. That's why he chooses them carefully.

> *If they transmit nothing more than that, the author has not chosen them carefully enough.*

In a book of the new art words don't transmit any intention; they're used to form a text which is an element of a book, and it is this book, as a totality, that transmits the author's intention.

> Do you want a world in which there are no authors, only book artists? No Melville, no Cervantes, and no Lope? Or do you mean that Cervantes and Lope ought to have no right to publish unless they print their books themselves?

•

Plagiarism is the starting point of the creative activity in the new art.

> In the really old art – oral literature – the emphasis was on shared cultural wealth rather than phony originality. Yet under those conditions, plenty of real originality and creativity shone through. Can the new art do as well?

Whenever the new art uses an isolated word, then it is in an absolute isolation: books of one single word.

> You continue to privilege space over time. And I continue to wonder why.

•

Old art's authors have the gift for language, the talent for language, the ease for language.

> Every author, old or new, needs a gift for language. And sooner or later every author worth his salt reaches the limit of that gift and has to start working.

For new art's authors language is an enigma, a problem; the book hints at ways to solve it.

> Are you sure the enigma of language needs a solution? If it does have a solution, is it really an enigma?

•

In the old art you write "I love you" thinking that this phrase means "I love you."

> If that's the only thing you write, you're a long way from writing a book.

(But: what does "I love you" mean?)

> It means "I love you."

•

In the new art you write "I love you" being aware that we don't know what this means. You write this phrase as part of a text wherein to write "I hate you" would come to the same thing.

You overstate your case.

The important thing is, that this phrase, "I love you" or "I hate you," performs a certain function as a text within the structure of the book.

Well, as you say, every structure is part of another. The language of the book is part of the larger structure of that language. The text of the book is part of the larger structure of literature. If the social life of humans is represented in that text, then larger structures of human life and psychology are also called into play. And in some of those structures there is something real which we call love. The text can refer to love just as it can to pine trees, radishes, and sunlight. All these things are real, though none of them are really in the book. What's in the book are words.

•

In the new art you don't love anybody.

If life imitates art, as so many people say, it might not be a good idea to banish love from art. But if all you really mean is that art and life are not the same, then I agree. The word 'pine' is not a pine tree. The word 'love' is not love. But when there is no love, the word has lost its meaning.

The old art claims to love.

The old art claims to represent reality, of which love is a real part.

In art you can love nobody. Only in real life can you love someone.

I do not think we really disagree here, yet I find your vehemence strange.

•

Not that the new art lacks passions.

Ah, but passion for what? For wisdom or for celebrity? For profundity of perception or glorification of the self?

All of it is blood flowing out of the wound that language has inflicted on men.

Again, I don't wish to be quarrelsome. But in what passes now for new art, that is not the wound that is bleeding most profusely.

And it is also the joy of being able to express something with everything, with anything, with almost nothing, with nothing.

Every now and then you make it sound as if the new art is a seamless continuation of the old.

•

The old art chooses, among the literary genres and forms, that one which best fits the author's intention.

When there is a road, old or new, that goes where you're going, you can travel on the road. When there isn't, you may have to bushwhack.

The new art uses any manifestation of language, since the author has no other intention than to test the language's ability to mean something.

You are trying to stage a fight between two partial statements of the truth. That is a fight which neither side can win, because neither side is whole.

•

The text of a book in the new art can be a novel as well as a single word, sonnets as well as jokes, love letters as well as weather reports.

All those things can be components in a work of literature. But if you mean to say that a telephone book or a weather report or a grocery list, or any single word, can be as nourishing as a work of literature, I say you are mistaken.

•

In the old art, just as the author's intention is ultimately unfathomable and the sense of his words indefinable, so the understanding of the reader is unquantifiable.

Are we the examination board? Why do we need to quantify the understanding of the reader?

In the new art the reading itself proves that the reader understands.

Reading proves nothing, just as writing proves nothing. It is the quality of the reading and writing that counts.

23

READING

In order to read the old art, knowing the alphabet is enough.

> Ha!

In order to read the new art one must apprehend the book as a structure, identifying its elements and understanding their function.

>> *You've heard about the man who said, "My grandmother ate with a fork, but because she mostly thought about the food and not the fork, she wasn't really eating. It's the fork that matters."*

>> •

One might read old art in the belief that one understands it, and be wrong.

> *One might do this with any art, old or new.*

Such a misunderstanding is impossible in the new art. You can read only if you understand.

> •

In the old art all books are read in the same way.

> *By whom?*

In the new art every book requires a different reading.

> *Every book that is a real book requires a different reading.*

> •

In the old art, to read the last page takes as much time as to read the first one.

>> *In any art that isn't fascist, readers are allowed to pause and savor anything they choose. This is a crucial difference between reading and performing. But there are also natural tempi. Just because the tempo isn't marked doesn't mean there is no tempo, nor that it doesn't change.*

In the new art the reading rhythm changes, quickens, speeds up.

>> *You mean there's one fixed pattern in this new art? One of the marks of a really good meal is often that the tempo slows toward the end.*

•

In order to understand and to appreciate a book of the old art, it is necessary to read it thoroughly.

>Let us hope.

In the new art you often do NOT need to read the whole book.

>Why then do you call it art?

The reading may stop at the very moment you have understood the total structure of the book.

>Do these works offer no continuing nourishment, then?

•

The new art makes it possible to read faster than the speed-reading methods.

>Why then do you call it art?

•

There are speed-reading methods because writing methods are too slow.

>You have this problem with time. But time is implicit in space, and vice versa.

•

The old art takes no heed of reading.

>Really?

The new art creates specific reading conditions.

>It conscripts the reader? Good thing, then, that the reader can read very quickly and needn't read to the end. But what's the point, except to show off?

•

The old art has even gone so far as to take the reader into account – which is going too far.

>It is said that when Herakleitos had written his book, he laid it down in the temple of Artemis. Did the goddess read it? Not that we know of. But humans are reading it

still, *even though human ignorance and greed have reduced it to fragments. Why do we read it? Because it fits the mind like a glove, like a comfortable shoe, and at the same time poses a challenge. That's what it means to take readers into account.*

·

The new art doesn't discriminate among its readers; it does not address itself to the book-addicts or try to steal its public away from TV.

Okay, no conscription. Just "conditions." But how is that different or new?

·

In order to be able to read the new art, and to understand it, you don't need to spend five years in a Faculty of English.

Literature has been around a good deal longer than the university. Sophocles and Aeschylus, Shakespeare and Cervantes, García Lorca and Neruda all had audiences who never sat in lecture halls or wrote examinations. And they have them still. But I'm not sure this new art of yours would ever have sprouted except on the fringes of the academy.

·

In order to be appreciated, the books of the new art don't need the senti-mental and/or intellectual complicity of their readers in matters of love, politics, psychology, geography, etc.

What, then, is the relation between these books and human life?

·

The new art appeals to the ability every man possesses for understanding and creating signs and systems of signs.

Is it really about technology, then?

·

CODE(X)+1 MONOGRAPH SERIES

CODE(X)+1 Series number one:
Robert Bringhurst. *Why there are pages and why they must turn.*
ISBN: 978-0-9817914-1-8 12 pp.

CODE(X)+1 Series number two:
Peter Rutledge Koch. *Art Definition Five and other writings.*
ISBN: 978-0-9817914-2-5 24 pp.

CODE(X)+1 Series number three:
Alan Loney. *each new book.*
ISBN: 978-0-9817914-3-2 24 pp.

CODE(X)+1 Series number four:
Ulrike Stoltz & Ute Schneider. *<usus>, typography, and artists' books.*
ISBN: 978-0-9817914-4-9 16 pp.

CODE(X)+1 Series number five:
Russell Maret. *Visionaries & Fanatics: type design & the private press.*
ISBN: 978-0-9817914-5-6 24 pp.

CODE(X)+1 Series number six:
Didier Mutel. *L'acide brut manifesto.*
ISBN: 978-0-9817914-6-3 24 pp.

CODE(X)+1 Series number seven:
Vincent Giroud. *Parole in libertà: Marinetti's Metal Book*
ISBN: 978-0-9817914-7-0 24 pp.

CODE(X)+1 Series number eight:
Filippo Tommaso Marinetti & Tullio D'albisola. *Parole in libertà futuriste olfattive tattili-termiche*
ISBN: 978-0-9817914-8-7 30 pp.

CODE(X)+1 Series number nine:
Karen Bleitz. *The Mechanical Word*
ISBN: 978-0-9817914-9-4 24 pp.

CODE(X)+1 Series number ten:
Monica Oppen. *This is not a Cathedral*
ISBN: 978-0-9962184-0-5 24 pp.

BOOK ART OBJECT

book art object
Documenting the first biennial Codex Book Fair & Symposium
735 color images
ISBN: 978-0-9817914-0-1 448 pp.

book art object 2
Documenting the third biennial Codex Book Fair & Symposium
1133 images of 300 books by 140 artists/printers
ISBN: 978-0-911221-50-3 524 pp.

IN CELEBRATION OF THE 5TH CODEX SYMPOSIUM, the 10th anniversary of the CODEX Foundation, and the 500th anniversary of the death of Aldus Manutius - we are pleased to announce *Alchimie du Verbe*, the first ever CODEX Assembly-Exchange; a carefully curated collection of printed works from some of the finest book artists and printers in the world.

Participating Artists:
Walter Bachinski & Janis Butler, Victoria Bean, Karen Bleitz, Carolee Campbell, Aaron Cohick, Crispin & Jan Elsted, Nacho Gallardo, Martha Hellion, Sarah Horowitz, Mikhail Karassik, Peter Rutledge Koch, Patricia Lagarde, Clemens-Tobias Lange, Alan Loney, Peter Malutski & Ines von Ketelhodt, Russell Maret, Rick Myers, Didier Mutel, Robin Price, Harry Reese & Sandra Liddell Reese, Dmitry Sayenko, Veronika Schapers, Gaylord Schanilec, Johannes Strugalla & Francoise Despalles, Richard Wagener, Sam Winston.

Individual copies $3500
To purchase, please see our website:
www.codexfoundation.org